THE GRAPH ISOMORPHISM ALGORITHM

ASHAY DHARWADKER

JOHN-TAGORE TEVET

ABSTRACT

We present a new polynomial-time algorithm for determining whether two given graphs are isomorphic or not. We prove that the algorithm is necessary and sufficient for solving the Graph Isomorphism Problem in polynomial-time, thus showing that the Graph Isomorphism Problem is in **P**. The semiotic theory for the recognition of graph structure is used to define a canonical form of the sign matrix of a graph. We prove that the canonical form of the sign matrix is uniquely identifiable in polynomial-time for isomorphic graphs. The algorithm is demonstrated by solving the Graph Isomorphism Problem for many of the hardest known examples. We implement the algorithm in C++ and provide a demonstration program for Microsoft Windows.

The Demonstration Program

http://www.dharwadker.org/tevet/isomorphism

CONTENTS

1. Introduction

One of the most fundamental problems in graph theory is the *Graph Isomorphism Problem*: given two graphs G_A and G_B, are they isomorphic? Graphs G_A and G_B are said to be *isomorphic* if their vertices can be rearranged so that the corresponding edge structure is exactly the same. To show that graphs G_A and G_B are isomorphic, it suffices to find one such rearrangement of vertices. On the other hand, to show that G_A and G_B are not isomorphic, one must prove that no such rearrangement of vertices can exist. Without a good algorithm, this problem can be very difficult to solve even for relatively small graphs.

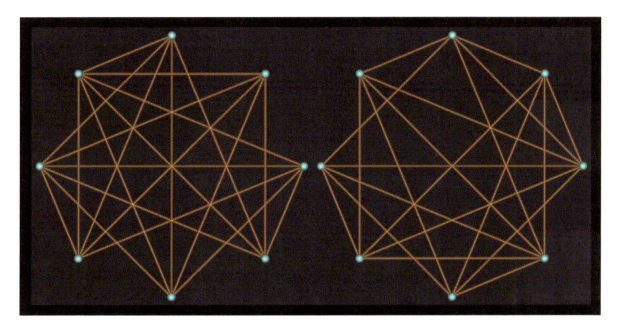

Figure 1.1. *Are graphs G_A and G_B isomorphic?*

We present a new polynomial-time **GRAPH ISOMORPHISM ALGORITHM** for determining whether two given graphs are isomorphic or not. If the given graphs are isomorphic, the algorithm finds an explicit isomorphism function in polynomial-time. In Section 2, we provide precise **DEFINITIONS** of all the terminology used and introduce the essential concept of a sign matrix according to the semiotic theory for the recognition of graph structure. In Section 3, we present a formal description of the **ALGORITHM** followed by an example to show how the algorithm works step-by-step. In Section 4, we prove that the algorithm is **NECESSARY AND SUFFICIENT** for solving the Graph Isomorphism Problem: if graphs G_A and G_B are isomorphic, then the algorithm finds an explicit isomorphism function; if graphs G_A and G_B are not isomorphic, then the algorithm determines that no isomorphism function can exist. In Section 5, we show that the algorithm has polynomial-time **COMPLEXITY**. Thus, we prove that the Graph Isomorphism Problem is in **P**. In Section 6, we provide an **IMPLEMENTATION** of the algorithm as a C++ program, together with demonstration software for Microsoft Windows. In Section 7, we demonstrate the algorithm by solving the Graph Isomorphism Problem for several **EXAMPLES** of graphs in the hardest known cases. In Section 8, we list the **REFERENCES**.

2. Definitions

To begin with, we present elementary definitions of all the terminology used, following **[1]**. Thereafter, we introduce the essential concept of a sign matrix according to the semiotic theory for the recognition of graph structure, following **[2]**.

A *finite simple graph* G consists of a set of *vertices* V, with $|V| = n$, and a set of *edges* E, such that each edge is an unordered pair of distinct vertices. The definition of a simple graph G forbids *loops* (edges joining a vertex to itself) and *multiple edges* (many edges joining a pair of vertices), whence the set E must also be finite, with $|E| = m$. We *label* the vertices of G with the integers $1, 2, ..., n$. If the unordered pair of vertices $\{u, v\}$ is an edge in G, we say that u is *adjacent* to v and write $uv \in E$. Adjacency is a symmetric relationship: $uv \in E$ if and only if $vu \in E$. The *degree* of a vertex v is the number of vertices that are adjacent to v. A (u, v)-*path* P in G is a sequence of distinct vertices $u = v_1, v_2, ..., v_k = v$ such that $v_i v_{i+1} \in E$ for $i = 1, 2, ..., k$-1. If such a (u, v)-path P exists, then the vertices u and v are said to be *connected* by a path of *length* k-1.

Given any pair of vertices (u, v) in G, we define the *distance*

$$d(u, v) = 0, \text{ if } u = v,$$

$$d(u, v) = \text{the length of a shortest } (u, v)\text{-path, if } u \text{ and } v \text{ are connected, and}$$

$$d(u, v) = \infty, \text{ otherwise.}$$

We now introduce the key ingredients of semiotic theory. For any pair of vertices (u, v) in G, the *collateral graph* $G \backslash uv$ is defined as follows:

- If $uv \in E$, then $G \backslash uv$ is obtained by deleting the edge uv from G while preserving all the vertices of G. We use the binary sign + to distinguish the distance function in this case.
- If $uv \notin E$, then $G \backslash uv = G$. We use the binary sign - to distinguish the distance function in this case.

The *pair graph* G_{uv} for any pair of vertices (u, v) in G is defined as follows:

- w is a vertex of G_{uv} if and only if w belongs to a shortest (u, v)-path in $G \backslash uv$, and
- wx is an edge of G_{uv} if and only if wx is also an edge of G.

For any pair of vertices (u, v) in G, we write the (u, v)-*sign*, denoted by the symbol s_{uv}, as follows:

$$s_{uv} = \pm \, d_{uv} \, . \, n_{uv} \, . \, m_{uv}$$

where

- the leading binary sign is positive if $uv \in E$, or negative if $uv \notin E$;
- d_{uv} is the distance $d(u, v)$ in the collateral graph $G \backslash uv$;
- n_{uv} is the number of vertices of the pair graph G_{uv};
- m_{uv} is the number of edges of the pair graph G_{uv}.

The *sign matrix S* of the graph G is written as an $n \times n$ array with the (u, v)-sign s_{uv} as the entry in row u and column v,

$$S = [\, s_{uv} \,] \, .$$

The *adjacency matrix* of G is an $n \times n$ matrix with the entry in row u and column v equal to 1 if $uv \in E$ and equal to 0 if $uv \notin E$. Thus, the adjacency matrix of the graph G can be recovered from the leading binary signs of the entries of the sign matrix S. Note that for a simple graph G, both the adjacency matrix and the sign matrix S are symmetric.

We shall now define a *canonical form S** of the sign matrix by ordering the rows and columns of S in a certain way. First, write the set of all distinct (u, v)-signs s_{uv} in lexicographic order $s_1, s_2, ..., s_r$. Then, for each row i of the sign matrix, $i = 1, 2, ..., n$, compute the *sign frequency vector*

$$f_i = (\, f_i^{(1)}, f_i^{(2)}, ..., f_i^{(r)} \,)$$

where $f_i^{(k)}$ is the number of times the sign s_k occurs in row i. Since S is symmetric, the sign frequency vector for column i is the same as the sign frequency vector for row i, for $i = 1, 2, ..., n$. Now, write the sign frequency vectors $f_1, f_2, ..., f_n$ in lexicographic order $f_{i_1}, f_{i_2}, ..., f_{i_n}$. Reorder the rows and columns of the sign matrix according to the permutation $i_1, i_2, ..., i_n$ of the vertices $1, 2, ..., n$ of G to obtain the canonical form S^* of the sign matrix.

The vertices of G are partitioned into *equivalence classes* consisting of vertices with the same sign frequency vectors. Thus, the canonical form S^* of the sign matrix is uniquely defined only upto permutations of vertices within each equivalence class.

Graphs G_A and G_B are said to be *isomorphic* if there exists a bijection

$$\varphi: V_A \rightarrow V_B$$

from the vertices of graph G_A to the vertices of graph G_B, such that uv is an edge in graph G_A if and only if $\varphi(u)\varphi(v)$ is an edge in graph G_B. The *graph isomorphism problem* is to determine whether two given graphs are isomorphic or not.

An *algorithm* is a problem-solving method suitable for implementation as a computer program.

While designing algorithms we are typically faced with a number of different approaches. For small problems, it hardly matters which approach we use, as long as it is one that solves the problem correctly. However, there are many problems for which the only known algorithms take so long to compute the solution that they are practically useless. For instance, the naïve approach of computing all $n!$ possible permutations of the n vertices to show that a pair of graphs G_A and G_B are not isomorphic is impractical even for small inputs.

A *polynomial-time algorithm* is one whose number of computational steps is always bounded by a polynomial function of the size of the input. Thus, a polynomial-time algorithm is one that is actually useful in practice. The class of all problems that have polynomial-time algorithms is denoted by **P**. If graphs G_A and G_B are isomorphic then they must have the same sign frequency vectors in lexicographic order $^fi_1, ^fi_2, ..., ^fi_n$ and we shall show that our algorithm obtains identical canonical forms of their sign matrices $S_A{}^*$ and $S_B{}^*$ in polynomial-time, thus exhibiting an explicit isomorphism function φ. Conversely, we shall show that our algorithm determines in polynomial-time that the sign matrices $S_A{}^*$ and $S_B{}^*$ cannot be expressed in identical canonical forms if and only if the graphs G_A and G_B are not isomorphic. Thus, we have a polynomial-time algorithm for solving the graph isomorphism problem, showing that the graph isomorphism problem is in **P**.

3. Algorithm

We are now ready to present a formal description of the algorithm. After that, the steps of the algorithm will be illustrated by an example. We begin by defining four procedures.

3.1. Procedure. This procedure is Dijkstra's algorithm [3]. Given a graph G and a vertex u, we compute shortest (u, v)-paths to all vertices v of G. Define $a(u, v) = 1$ if $uv \in E$ and $a(u, v) = \infty$ if $uv \notin E$. We maintain a set V_{known} of vertices to which the shortest (u, v)-path is known and a tentative distance $d'(u, w)$ for each vertex w outside V_{known}.

- **Initialization:** Set $V_{known} = \{u\}$, $d(u, u) = 0$ and $d'(u, w) = a(u, w)$ for each vertex w outside V_{known}.
- **Iteration:** Select a vertex w_{min} outside V_{known} such that $d'(u, w_{min})$ is a minimum. Add w_{min} to V_{known} and update the tentative distance $d'(u, w) = \min\{d'(u, w), d(u, w) + a(u, w)\}$ for each vertex w outside V_{known}.
- **Termination:** Iterate until V_{known} contains all the vertices of G or until $d'(u, w) = \infty$ for each vertex w outside V_{known}. In the later case, no further vertex can be selected and the remaining vertices are not connected to the vertex u.

3.2. Procedure. Given a graph G and vertices u and v, we compute the distance $d(u, v)$ in the collateral graph $G \backslash uv$ and the pair graph G_{uv}.

- Using Procedure 3.1, compute shortest (u, x)-paths to all vertices x of $G \backslash uv$.
- Using Procedure 3.1, compute shortest (v, y)-paths to all vertices y of $G \backslash uv$.

8

- In particular, the length of any shortest (u, v)-path in $G \backslash uv$ is the distance $d(u, v)$.
- If $u = u_1, u_2, ..., u_r$ and $v = v_1, v_2, ..., v_s$ are shortest paths found above such that $u_r = v_s$ and the sum of the lengths of the two paths is the distance $d(u, v)$ in the collateral graph $G \backslash uv$, then the union of vertices of the two paths are vertices of the pair graph G_{uv}. Every vertex w of the pair graph G_{uv} is obtained this way, because any shortest (u, v)-path containing w is obtained by connecting some shortest (u, w)-path with some shortest (w, v)-path in $G \backslash uv$. Thus, at least one pair of shortest paths found above must satisfy $u_r = v_s = w$, for each vertex w of the pair graph G_{uv}.

3.3. Procedure. Given a graph G, we compute the sign matrix S and its canonical form S^*.

- Using Procedure 3.2, for every pair of vertices u and v, we compute the distance $d(u, v)$ in the collateral graph $G \backslash uv$ and the pair graph G_{uv}.
- The entry in row u and column v of the sign matrix S is $s_{uv} = \pm d_{uv}.n_{uv}.m_{uv}$, where the leading binary sign is positive if $uv \in E$, and negative if $uv \notin E$; d_{uv} is the distance $d(u, v)$ in the collateral graph $G \backslash uv$; n_{uv} is the number of vertices of the pair graph G_{uv}; and m_{uv} is the number of edges of the pair graph G_{uv}.
- Write the set of all distinct signs s_{uv} in lexicographic order $s_1, s_2, ..., s_r$.
- For each row i of the sign matrix S, $i = 1, 2, ..., n$, compute the sign frequency vector $f_i = (f_i^{(1)}, f_i^{(2)}, ..., f_i^{(r)})$, where $f_i^{(k)}$ is the number of times the sign s_k occurs in row i. Since S is symmetric, the sign frequency vector for column i is the same as the sign frequency vector for row i, for $i = 1, 2, ..., n$.
- Write the sign frequency vectors $f_1, f_2, ..., f_n$ in lexicographic order $f_{i_1}, f_{i_2}, ..., f_{i_n}$.
- Reorder the rows and columns of the sign matrix according to the permutation $i_1, i_2, ..., i_n$ of the vertices $1, 2, ..., n$ of G to obtain the canonical form S^*.

3.4. Procedure. Given graphs G_A and G_B such that the sign frequency vectors in lexicographic order for S_A^* and S_B^* are the same, ($f_{Ai_1}, f_{Ai_2}, ..., f_{Ai_n}$) = ($f_{Bi'_1}, f_{Bi'_2}, ..., f_{Bi'_n}$), we compute a reordering $i''_1, i''_2, ..., i''_n$ of the vertices of G_B such that either the first entry of S_B^* that does not match the corresponding entry of S_A^* occurs at the greatest possible index in row major order or $S_A^* = S_B^*$.

- Set $A = S_A^*$ and $B = S_B^*$.
- Read the matrices A and B in row major order (read each row from left to right and read the rows from top to bottom). If all corresponding entries A_{ij} and B_{ij} of A and B match, then stop. Else, find the first entry B_{ij} in B that does not match the corresponding entry A_{ij} in A. Find $k > i$ such that interchanging rows (k, j) and columns (k, j) of B ensures that the first mismatch occurs later than B_{ij} in row major order (or there is no mismatch at all). If no such k exists, then stop. Repeat this process until the corresponding k cannot be found or all corresponding entries of A and B match.
- We obtain a reordering $i''_1, i''_2, ..., i''_n$ of the vertices of G_B such that either the first entry of B that does not match the corresponding entry of A occurs at the greatest possible index in row major order or $A = B$.

3.5. Algorithm. Given graphs G_A and G_B, we determine whether G_A and G_B are isomorphic or not. If G_A and G_B are isomorphic, we exhibit an explicit isomorphism function.

- Using Procedure 3.3, we compute the canonical forms of the sign matrices S_A* and S_B*. If the sign frequency vectors in lexicographic order for S_A* and S_B* are different, then G_A and G_B are not isomorphic and we stop.
- Else, the sign frequency vectors in lexicographic order for S_A* and S_B* are the same, ($^f{}_Ai_1, ^f{}_Ai_2, ..., ^f{}_Ai_n$) = ($^f{}_Bi'_1, ^f{}_Bi'_2, ..., ^f{}_Bi'_n$).
    - For $k = 1, 2, ..., n$:
        - Set $A = S_A*$ and $B = S_B*$.
        - Interchange rows $(1, k)$ and columns $(1, k)$ of B.
        - Using Procedure 3.4, if $A = B$ then stop. Else, start with the next value of k. If $k = n$ then stop.
    - If $A \neq B$, then G_A and G_B are not isomorphic. Else $A = B$, G_A and G_B are isomorphic and the reordering $i''_1, i''_2, ..., i''_n$ of the vertices of G_B to obtain $S_B* = B$ provides an explicit isomorphism function $\varphi(i_1) = i''_1, \varphi(i_2) = i''_2, ..., \varphi(i_n) = i''_n$.

3.6. Example. We demonstrate the steps of the algorithm with an example. The input consists of Turán **[4]** graphs G_A and G_B, with vertices labeled $V_A = \{1, 2, 3, 4, 5, 6, 7, 8\}$ and $V_B = \{1, 2, 3, 4, 5, 6, 7, 8\}$ as shown below in Figure 3.6.1.

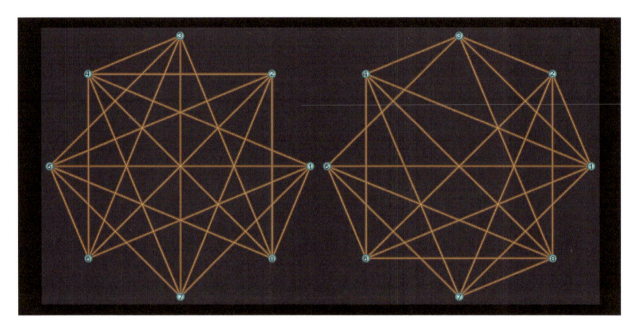

Figure 3.6.1. *An example to demonstrate the steps of the algorithm : input*

The algorithm first computes all the pair graphs of G_A. To see how this is done, let us explicitly compute the pair graph G_{12} for the pair of vertices (1, 2). First, Procedure 3.2 computes the shortest paths from vertex 1 in $G_A\backslash 12$ as (1), (1, 7, 2), (1, 7, 3), (1, 7), (1, 8), (1, 4), (1, 5) and (1, 6). Then, Procedure 3.2 computes the shortest paths from vertex 2 in $G_A\backslash 12$

as (2), (2, 7, 1), (2, 7, 3), (2, 7), (2, 8), (2, 4), (2, 5) and (2, 6). The distance $d(1, 2) = 2$ is given by the length of any shortest (1, 2)-path found in $G_A\backslash 12$ so far. Now, Procedure 3.2 obtains the shortest (1, 2)-paths (1, 7, 2), (1, 8, 2), (1, 4, 2), (1, 5, 2) and (1, 6, 2) whose union gives the 7 vertices of the pair graph {1, 2, 4, 5, 6, 7, 8}. The pair graph has 16 edges {1,7}, {1,8}, {1,4}, {1,5}, {1,6}, {2,7}, {2,8}, {2,4}, {2,5}, {2,6}, {7,4}, {7,5}, {8,4}, {8,5}, {4,6} and {5,6}. Since {1, 2} is not an edge in G_A, the leading binary sign is negative and Procedure 3.3 computes the sign $s_{12} = $ -2.7.16. Similarly, Procedure 3.3 computes all the signs s_{ij} for $i, j = 1, 2, 3, 4, 5, 6, 7, 8$. Note that for $i = j$ the sign is always -0.1.0. Thus, Procedure 3.3 computes the sign matrix S_A. Then, Procedure 3.3 counts the number of times each sign occurs in a column of S_A and obtains the sign frequency vectors for each column of S_A. Finally, Procedure 3.3 reorders the rows and columns of S_A according to the lexicographic order of the sign frequency vectors, to obtain the canonical form of the sign matrix S_A*. We use the following convention to display the sign matrix: the row and column headers show the vertex labels and the equivalence classes of vertices are distinguished by different shades of blue; the sign frequency vectors, vertex degrees and equivalence class numbers are displayed along the column footers.

S_A*	4	5	1	2	3	7	8	6
4	-0.1.0	-2.8.21	+2.5.7	+2.5.7	+2.5.7	+2.5.7	+2.5.7	+2.5.7
5	-2.8.21	-0.1.0	+2.5.7	+2.5.7	+2.5.7	+2.5.7	+2.5.7	+2.5.7
1	+2.5.7	+2.5.7	-0.1.0	-2.7.16	-2.7.16	+2.4.5	+2.4.5	+2.4.5
2	+2.5.7	+2.5.7	-2.7.16	-0.1.0	-2.7.16	+2.4.5	+2.4.5	+2.4.5
3	+2.5.7	+2.5.7	-2.7.16	-2.7.16	-0.1.0	+2.4.5	+2.4.5	+2.4.5
7	+2.5.7	+2.5.7	+2.4.5	+2.4.5	+2.4.5	-0.1.0	-2.7.16	-2.7.16
8	+2.5.7	+2.5.7	+2.4.5	+2.4.5	+2.4.5	-2.7.16	-0.1.0	-2.7.16
6	+2.5.7	+2.5.7	+2.4.5	+2.4.5	+2.4.5	-2.7.16	-2.7.16	-0.1.0
Signs	4	5	1	2	3	7	8	6
-2.7.16.	0	0	2	2	2	2	2	2
-2.8.21.	1	1	0	0	0	0	0	0
-0.1.0.	1	1	1	1	1	1	1	1
+2.4.5.	0	0	3	3	3	3	3	3
+2.5.7.	6	6	2	2	2	2	2	2
Degrees	6	6	5	5	5	5	5	5
Classes	1	1	2	2	2	2	2	2

Similarly, Procedure 3.3 obtains the canonical form of the sign matrix S_B* :

S_B*	1	8	7	2	3	4	5	6
1	-0.1.0	-2.8.21	+2.5.7	+2.5.7	+2.5.7	+2.5.7	+2.5.7	+2.5.7
8	-2.8.21	-0.1.0	+2.5.7	+2.5.7	+2.5.7	+2.5.7	+2.5.7	+2.5.7
7	+2.5.7	+2.5.7	-0.1.0	+2.4.5	-2.7.16	+2.4.5	+2.4.5	-2.7.16
2	+2.5.7	+2.5.7	+2.4.5	-0.1.0	+2.4.5	-2.7.16	-2.7.16	+2.4.5
3	+2.5.7	+2.5.7	-2.7.16	+2.4.5	-0.1.0	+2.4.5	+2.4.5	-2.7.16
4	+2.5.7	+2.5.7	+2.4.5	-2.7.16	+2.4.5	-0.1.0	-2.7.16	+2.4.5
5	+2.5.7	+2.5.7	+2.4.5	-2.7.16	+2.4.5	-2.7.16	-0.1.0	+2.4.5
6	+2.5.7	+2.5.7	-2.7.16	+2.4.5	-2.7.16	+2.4.5	+2.4.5	-0.1.0
Signs	1	8	7	2	3	4	5	6
-2.7.16.	0	0	2	2	2	2	2	2
-2.8.21.	1	1	0	0	0	0	0	0
-0.1.0.	1	1	1	1	1	1	1	1
+2.4.5.	0	0	3	3	3	3	3	3
+2.5.7.	6	6	2	2	2	2	2	2
Degrees	6	6	5	5	5	5	5	5
Classes	1	1	2	2	2	2	2	2

Next, the algorithm checks that the sign frequency vectors in lexicographic order for S_A* and S_B* are the same,

$$({}^f_A4, {}^f_A5, {}^f_A1, {}^f_A2, {}^f_A3, {}^f_A7, {}^f_A8, {}^f_A6) = ({}^f_B1, {}^f_B8, {}^f_B7, {}^f_B3, {}^f_B6, {}^f_B4, {}^f_B5, {}^f_B2)$$

$$= (01106, 01106, 20132, 20132, 20132, 20132, 20132, 20132).$$

Finally, the algorithm runs through the loop $k = 1, 2, 3, 4, 5, 6, 7, 8$ to find an explicit isomorphism if it exists. Starting with $k = 1$, set $A = S_A{}^*$ and $B = S_B{}^*$:

Matrix A	4	5	1	2	3	7	8	6
4	-0.1.0	-2.8.21	+2.5.7	+2.5.7	+2.5.7	+2.5.7	+2.5.7	+2.5.7
5	-2.8.21	-0.1.0	+2.5.7	+2.5.7	+2.5.7	+2.5.7	+2.5.7	+2.5.7
1	+2.5.7	+2.5.7	-0.1.0	-2.7.16	-2.7.16	+2.4.5	+2.4.5	+2.4.5
2	+2.5.7	+2.5.7	-2.7.16	-0.1.0	-2.7.16	+2.4.5	+2.4.5	+2.4.5
3	+2.5.7	+2.5.7	-2.7.16	-2.7.16	-0.1.0	+2.4.5	+2.4.5	+2.4.5
7	+2.5.7	+2.5.7	+2.4.5	+2.4.5	+2.4.5	-0.1.0	-2.7.16	-2.7.16
8	+2.5.7	+2.5.7	+2.4.5	+2.4.5	+2.4.5	-2.7.16	-0.1.0	-2.7.16
6	+2.5.7	+2.5.7	+2.4.5	+2.4.5	+2.4.5	-2.7.16	-2.7.16	-0.1.0

Matrix B	1	8	7	2	3	4	5	6
1	-0.1.0	-2.8.21	+2.5.7	+2.5.7	+2.5.7	+2.5.7	+2.5.7	+2.5.7
8	-2.8.21	-0.1.0	+2.5.7	+2.5.7	+2.5.7	+2.5.7	+2.5.7	+2.5.7
7	+2.5.7	+2.5.7	-0.1.0	<u>+2.4.5</u>	-2.7.16	+2.4.5	+2.4.5	-2.7.16
2	+2.5.7	+2.5.7	+2.4.5	-0.1.0	+2.4.5	-2.7.16	-2.7.16	+2.4.5
3	+2.5.7	+2.5.7	-2.7.16	+2.4.5	-0.1.0	+2.4.5	+2.4.5	-2.7.16
4	+2.5.7	+2.5.7	+2.4.5	-2.7.16	+2.4.5	-0.1.0	-2.7.16	+2.4.5
5	+2.5.7	+2.5.7	+2.4.5	-2.7.16	+2.4.5	-2.7.16	-0.1.0	+2.4.5
6	+2.5.7	+2.5.7	-2.7.16	+2.4.5	-2.7.16	+2.4.5	+2.4.5	-0.1.0

Since $k = 1$, there is no initial interchange of rows and columns of B. Now, the algorithm uses Procedure 3.4. The entries of A and B are read in row major order. The first mismatch is found in the third row and fourth column, shown underlined. The algorithm finds that exchanging the fourth column with the fifth column (and the fourth row with the fifth row) of B will push the first mismatch further along the row major order:

Matrix B	1	8	7	3	2	4	5	6
1	-0.1.0	-2.8.21	+2.5.7	+2.5.7	+2.5.7	+2.5.7	+2.5.7	+2.5.7
8	-2.8.21	-0.1.0	+2.5.7	+2.5.7	+2.5.7	+2.5.7	+2.5.7	+2.5.7
7	+2.5.7	+2.5.7	-0.1.0	-2.7.16	<u>+2.4.5</u>	+2.4.5	+2.4.5	-2.7.16
3	+2.5.7	+2.5.7	-2.7.16	-0.1.0	+2.4.5	+2.4.5	+2.4.5	-2.7.16
2	+2.5.7	+2.5.7	+2.4.5	+2.4.5	-0.1.0	-2.7.16	-2.7.16	+2.4.5
4	+2.5.7	+2.5.7	+2.4.5	+2.4.5	-2.7.16	-0.1.0	-2.7.16	+2.4.5
5	+2.5.7	+2.5.7	+2.4.5	+2.4.5	-2.7.16	-2.7.16	-0.1.0	+2.4.5
6	+2.5.7	+2.5.7	-2.7.16	-2.7.16	+2.4.5	+2.4.5	+2.4.5	-0.1.0

The first mismatch is found in the third row and fifth column, shown underlined. The algorithm finds that exchanging the fifth column with the eighth column (and the fifth row with the eighth row) of B will push the first mismatch further along the row major order:

Matrix B	1	8	7	3	6	4	5	2
1	-0.1.0	-2.8.21	+2.5.7	+2.5.7	+2.5.7	+2.5.7	+2.5.7	+2.5.7
8	-2.8.21	-0.1.0	+2.5.7	+2.5.7	+2.5.7	+2.5.7	+2.5.7	+2.5.7
7	+2.5.7	+2.5.7	-0.1.0	-2.7.16	-2.7.16	+2.4.5	+2.4.5	+2.4.5
3	+2.5.7	+2.5.7	-2.7.16	-0.1.0	-2.7.16	+2.4.5	+2.4.5	+2.4.5
6	+2.5.7	+2.5.7	-2.7.16	-2.7.16	-0.1.0	+2.4.5	+2.4.5	+2.4.5
4	+2.5.7	+2.5.7	+2.4.5	+2.4.5	+2.4.5	-0.1.0	-2.7.16	-2.7.16
5	+2.5.7	+2.5.7	+2.4.5	+2.4.5	+2.4.5	-2.7.16	-0.1.0	-2.7.16
2	+2.5.7	+2.5.7	+2.4.5	+2.4.5	+2.4.5	-2.7.16	-2.7.16	-0.1.0

Now there is no mismatch, $A = B$. The algorithm exits the final loop and reports that an isomorphism has been found. The explicit isomorphism φ is given by reading the vertex labels of A and B in this order:

Graph G_A	Graph G_B
4	1
5	8
1	7
2	3
3	6
7	4
8	5
6	2

If the graphs G_A and G_B are redrawn with vertices ordered in this way, the isomorphism φ is easy to visualize.

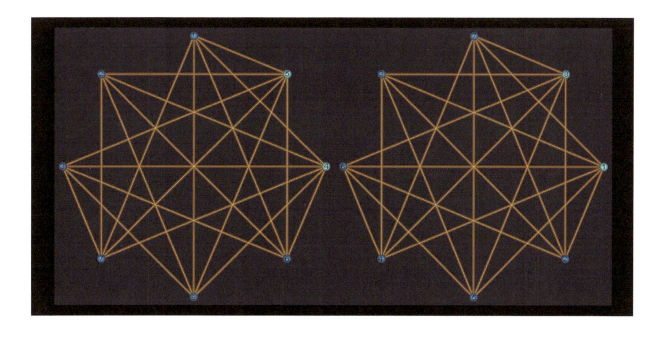

Figure 3.6.2. An example to demonstrate the steps of the algorithm : output

15

4. Necessity and Sufficiency

Here we prove that the algorithm is necessary and sufficient for solving the Graph Isomorphism Problem:

- if graphs G_A and G_B are isomorphic, then the algorithm finds an explicit isomorphism function;
- if graphs G_A and G_B are not isomorphic, then the algorithm determines that no isomorphism function can exist.

4.1. Proposition. If graphs G_A and G_B are isomorphic, then the algorithm finds an isomorphism.

Proof. Suppose graphs G_A and G_B are isomorphic and let $\varphi: V_A \to V_B$ be an isomorphism from the vertices of G_A to the vertices of G_B. Note that distances are preserved bijectively under the isomorphism,

$$d(u, v) = d(\varphi(u), \varphi(v))$$

for all vertices u, v of G_A. Thus, all the corresponding pair graphs are isomorphic and the signs

$$s_{uv} = s_{\varphi(u)\varphi(v)}$$

are also preserved bijectively under the isomorphism for all vertices u, v of G_A. Hence, the sign frequency vectors in lexicographic order for the canonical sign matrices $S_A{}^*$ and $S_B{}^*$ are the same,

$$({}^f_A i_1, {}^f_A i_2, ..., {}^f_A i_n) = ({}^f_B i'_1, {}^f_B i'_2, ..., {}^f_B i'_n).$$

Since φ is surjective, the algorithm finds a value of k such that if vertex v_1 is the label of row 1 and column 1 of $A = S_A{}^*$ then vertex $\varphi(v_1)$ is the label of row k and column k of $B = S_B{}^*$. Then, rows $(1, k)$ and columns $(1, k)$ of B are interchanged. We now use induction on the rows of B to show that Procedure 3.4 matches each row of B with the corresponding row of A. For the base of the induction, consider row 1 of B. Since vertex v_1 is the label of row 1 of A and $\varphi(v_1)$ is the label of row 1 of B, the corresponding sign frequency vectors are equal. By counting sign frequencies, as long as there is a mismatch in row 1, it is always possible to interchange the columns of B such that row 1 of A and row 1 of B are perfectly matched by Procedure 3.4. For the induction hypothesis, assume that rows 1, ..., t of A and B have been perfectly matched

16

by Procedure 3.4 such that the vertex labels for the rows 1, ..., t of A are v_1, ..., v_t and the vertex labels for the rows 1, ..., t of B are $\varphi(v_1) = v'_1$, ..., $\varphi(v_t) = v'_t$ respectively. Since the sign matrices are symmetric, Procedure 3.4 also ensures that the columns 1, ..., t of A and B are perfectly matched with the same vertex labels as the rows. Thus, the first entry B_{ij} in B that does not match the corresponding entry A_{ij} in A must now occur in row $i = t+1$ and column $j \geq t+1$. By the induction hypothesis, the subgraph G_A^t of G_A with vertices $\{v_1, ..., v_t\}$ and the subgraph G_B^t of G_B with vertices $\{\varphi(v_1) = v'_1, ..., \varphi(v_t) = v'_t\}$ are isomorphic under φ. Thus, there must be a vertex v_{t+1} of G_A outside the subgraph G_A^t such that the corresponding vertex $\varphi(v_{t+1})$ of G_B is outside the subgraph G_B^t. Since there is a mismatch at the entry B_{ij}, the vertex $\varphi(v_{t+1})$ must be the label for a column j' > j. Hence, Procedure 3.4 will always interchange rows (j, j') and columns (j, j') of B and repeat the process until rows $i = t+1$ of A and B are perfectly matched and the vertex label for row $t+1$ of B is $\varphi(v_{t+1}) = v'_{t+1}$. This completes the induction, showing that Procedure 3.4 matches each row of B with the corresponding row of A. Thus, the algorithm finds an explicit isomorphism function $\varphi(v_1) = v'_1$, ..., $\varphi(v_n) = v'_n$. $\square$

4.2. Proposition. If graphs G_A and G_B are not isomorphic, then the algorithm determines that there cannot be an isomorphism.

Proof. Suppose graphs G_A and G_B are not isomorphic. The algorithm first computes the canonical forms of the sign matrices $S_A{}^*$ and $S_B{}^*$. If the sign frequency vectors in lexicographic order for $S_A{}^*$ and $S_B{}^*$ are different, then the algorithm concludes that G_A and G_B are not isomorphic. If the sign frequency vectors in lexicographic order for $S_A{}^*$ and $S_B{}^*$ are the same, ($^f\!A_{i1}, {}^f\!A_{i2}, ..., {}^f\!A_{in}$) = ($^f\!B_{i'1}, {}^f\!B_{i'2}, ..., {}^f\!B_{i'n}$), then the algorithm runs through the final loop for $k = 1, 2, ..., n$ and cannot find any isomorphism. By Proposition 4.1, if G_A and G_B were isomorphic, then the algorithm would have found an explicit isomorphism for some value of k. Therefore, the algorithm concludes that there cannot be an isomorphism. $\square$

From Propositions 4.1 and 4.2, we have

4.3. Theorem. The algorithm solves the Graph Isomorphism Problem. $\square$

5. Complexity

We shall now show that the algorithm terminates in polynomial-time, by specifying a polynomial of the larger of the two number of vertices n of the input graphs, that is an upper bound on the total number of computational steps performed by the algorithm. Note that we consider

- checking whether a given pair of vertices is connected by an edge in G_A or G_B, and

- comparing whether a given integer is less than another given integer

to be *elementary computational steps*. Thus, we shall show that the Graph Isomorphism Problem is in **P**.

5.1. Proposition. Given a graph G with n vertices, Procedure 3.1 takes at most $3n^2 + 3n$ steps to find shortest paths from an initial vertex u to all other vertices.

Proof. Initialization takes at most $3n$ steps. To find the minimum distance of an unknown vertex from the initial vertex u takes at most n steps and to update the tentative distances takes at most n steps. There are at most n iterations until all the vertices are known. Finally, it takes at most n^2 steps to recover the vertices of the shortest paths. Thus, Procedure 3.1 terminates after at most $3n + n(n + n) + n^2 = 3n^2 + 3n$ steps. $\square$

5.2. Proposition. Given a graph G with n vertices, Procedure 3.2 takes at most $7n^2 + 7n$ steps to compute the distance $d(u, v)$ in the collateral graph $G\backslash uv$ and the pair graph G_{uv} for a given pair of vertices u and v.

Proof. The graph $G\backslash uv$ also has n vertices. By Proposition 5.1, Procedure 3.1 takes at most $3n^2 + 3n$ steps to find shortest paths from the initial vertex u to all other vertices and at most $3n^2 + 3n$ steps to find shortest paths from the initial vertex v to all other vertices. Then it takes at most n steps to determine the distance $d(u, v)$. Finally, it takes at most n^2 steps to run through pairs of shortest paths to find the vertices of the pair graph G_{uv}. Thus, Procedure 3.2 terminates after at most $3n^2 + 3n + 3n^2 + 3n + n + n^2 = 7n^2 + 7n$ steps. $\square$

5.3. Proposition. Given a graph G with n vertices, Procedure 3.3 takes at most $7n^4 + 7n^3 + 2n^2$ steps to compute the canonical form of the sign matrix S^*.

Proof. By Proposition 5.2, for each pair of vertices it takes at most $7n^2 + 7n$ steps to compute the sign s_{uv}. Since there are n^2 signs, it takes at most $n^2(7n^2 + 7n) = 7n^4 + 7n^3$ steps to compute the sign matrix S. Then it takes at most n^2 steps to compute the sign frequency vector and at most n^2 steps to sort it in lexicographic order. Thus, Procedure 3.3 terminates after at most $7n^4 + 7n^3 + n^2 + n^2 = 7n^4 + 7n^3 + 2n^2$ steps. $\square$

5.4. Proposition. Given a sign matrices S_A^* and S_B^* such that the sign frequency vectors in lexicographic order ($^f_A i_1$, $^f_A i_2$, ..., $^f_A i_n$) = ($^f_B i'_1$, $^f_B i'_2$, ..., $^f_B i'_n$), Procedure 3.4 takes at most $2n^4$ steps to terminate.

Proof. Since there are n^2 entries in S_B^*, it takes at most n^2 steps to find a mismatch (i, j) with the corresponding entry in S_A^* in row major order. Then, it takes at most n^2 steps along the row i to find a column j' such that interchanging rows (j, j') and columns (j, j') leads to a mismatch later in the row major order. This may be repeated at most n^2

18

times until either the corresponding interchange column j' cannot be found or all the entries in the sign matrices are perfectly matched. Thus, Procedure 3.4 terminates after at most $n^2(n^2 + n^2) = 2n^4$ steps. $\square$

5.5. Proposition. Given graphs G_A and G_B with n vertices, the algorithm takes at most $2n^5 + 14n^4 + 14n^3 + 4n^2$ steps to terminate.

Proof. By Proposition 5.3, Procedure 3.3 takes at most $2(7n^4 + 7n^3 + 2n^2) = 14n^4 + 14n^3 + 4n^2$ steps to compute the canonical forms of the sign matrices S_A* and S_B*. If the sign frequency vectors in lexicographic order (f_{Ai_1}, f_{Ai_2}, ..., f_{Ai_n}) = ($f_{Bi'_1}$, $f_{Bi'_2}$, ..., $f_{Bi'_n}$) are the same, then by Proposition 5.4 the final loop for $k = 1, 2, ..., n$ takes at most $n(2n^4) = 2n^5$ steps. Thus, the algorithm terminates after at most $2n^5 + 14n^4 + 14n^3 + 4n^2$ steps. $\square$

From Theorem 4.3 and Proposition 5.5, we have

5.6. Theorem. The Graph Isomorphism Problem is in **P**. $\square$

6. Implementation

We provide a demonstration program for the Graph Isomorphism Algorithm written in *C++* for Microsoft Windows. The input consists of the files *Graph A.txt* and *Graph B.txt* containing the adjacency matrices of graph G_A and graph G_B respectively. The program computes the sign matrices S_A* and S_B* in canonical form and determines whether G_A and G_B are isomorphic or not, in polynomial-time.

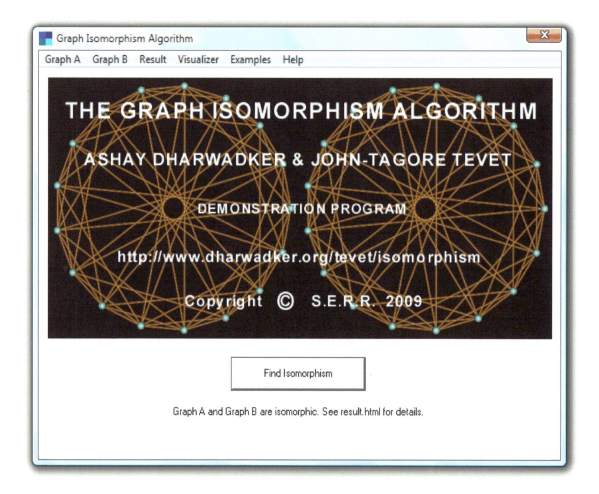

Figure 6.1. *A demonstration program for Microsoft Windows* **[download]**

We show how to write the input for the computation performed in Example 3.6:

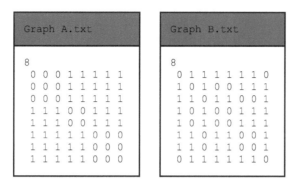

Figure 6.2. Input for the demonstration program

The *C*++ program is shown below:

```
isororphism.cpp

#include <iostream>
#include <fstream>
#include <string>
#include <vector>
#include <map>
#include <set>
#include <algorithm>
using namespace std;

vector<vector<int> > dijkstra(vector<vector<int> > graph);
vector<vector<int> > reindex(vector<vector<int> > graph, vector<int> index);
vector<int> inv(vector<int> index);
vector<int> transform(map<vector<int>,vector<int> > signmatrixA,
map<vector<int>,vector<int> > signmatrixB, vector<int> vertexA,
vector<int> vertexB, vector<int> isoB);
ifstream infileA("graphA.txt");
ifstream infileB("graphB.txt");
ofstream outfile("result.txt");

int main()
{
cout<<"The Graph Isomorphism Algorithm"<<endl;
cout<<"by Ashay Dharwadker and John-Tagore Tevet"<<endl;
cout<<"http://www.geocities.com/dharwadker/tevet/isomorphism/"<<endl;
cout<<"Copyright (c) 2009"<<endl;
```

Figure 6.3. A *C*++ program for the graph isomorphism algorithm **[download]**

21

The output of the program for the input in Figure 6.2 is shown in Example 3.6. The next section shows many more examples of input/output files. The download package also contains a visualizer for drawing graphs according to the output of the demonstration program.

7. Examples

We now demonstrate the Graph Isomorphism Algorithm for several examples. The first set of examples 7.1-7.5 consists of isomorphic graphs whose vertices have been permuted randomly so that the isomorphism is well and truly hidden. The second set of examples 7.6-7.9 consists of graphs that are not isomorphic and yet have a very similar structure, hence deciding that they are not isomorphic in polynomial-time demonstrates the power of the algorithm.

7.1. Example. We run the program on isomorphic Petersen [5] graphs A and B as input:

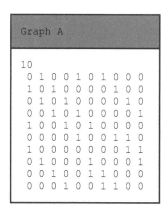

```
Graph A

10
 0 1 0 0 1 0 1 0 0 0
 1 0 1 0 0 0 0 1 0 0
 0 1 0 1 0 0 0 0 1 0
 0 0 1 0 1 0 0 0 0 1
 1 0 0 1 0 1 0 0 0 0
 0 0 0 0 1 0 0 1 1 0
 1 0 0 0 0 0 0 0 1 1
 0 1 0 0 0 1 0 0 0 1
 0 0 1 0 0 1 1 0 0 0
 0 0 0 1 0 0 1 1 0 0
```

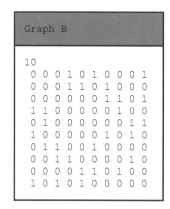

```
Graph B

10
 0 0 0 1 0 1 0 0 0 1
 0 0 0 1 1 0 1 0 0 0
 0 0 0 0 0 0 1 1 0 1
 1 1 0 0 0 0 0 1 0 0
 0 1 0 0 0 0 0 0 1 1
 1 0 0 0 0 0 1 0 1 0
 0 1 1 0 0 1 0 0 0 0
 0 0 1 1 0 0 0 0 1 0
 0 0 0 0 1 1 0 1 0 0
 1 0 1 0 1 0 0 0 0 0
```

22

The algorithm finds an explicit isomorphism, shown below.

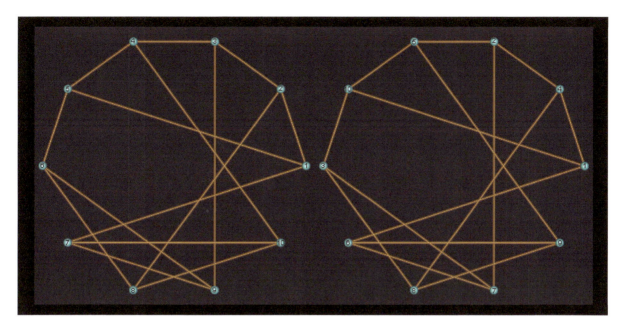

Figure 7.1. *The Petersen graphs are isomorphic*

7.2. Example. We run the program on isomorphic Icosahedron [6] graphs A and B as input:

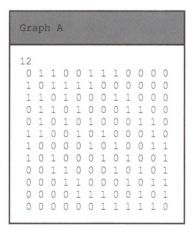

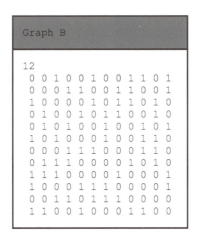

```
Graph B

12
 0 0 1 0 0 1 0 0 1 1 0 1
 0 0 0 1 1 0 0 1 1 0 0 1
 1 0 0 0 0 1 0 1 1 0 1 0
 0 1 0 0 1 0 1 1 0 0 1 0
 0 1 0 1 0 0 1 0 0 1 0 1
 1 0 1 0 0 0 1 0 0 1 1 0
 0 0 0 1 1 1 0 0 0 1 1 0
 0 1 1 1 0 0 0 0 1 0 1 0
 1 1 1 0 0 0 1 0 0 0 0 1
 1 0 0 0 1 1 1 0 0 0 0 1
 0 0 1 1 0 1 1 1 0 0 0 0
 1 1 0 0 1 0 0 0 1 1 0 0
```

The algorithm finds an explicit isomorphism, shown below.

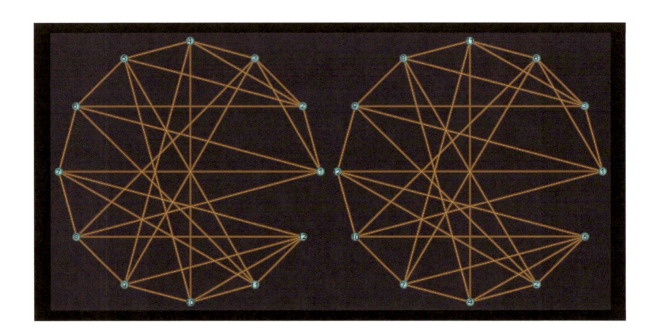

Figure 7.2. *The Icosahedron graphs are isomorphic*

24

7.3. Example. We run the program on isomorphic Ramsey [7] graphs A and B as input:

```
Graph A

17
0 1 1 0 1 0 0 0 1 1 0 0 0 1 0 1 1
1 0 1 1 0 1 0 0 0 1 1 0 0 0 1 0 1
1 1 0 1 1 0 1 0 0 0 1 1 0 0 0 1 0
0 1 1 0 1 1 0 1 0 0 0 1 1 0 0 0 1
1 0 1 1 0 1 1 0 1 0 0 0 1 1 0 0 0
0 1 0 1 1 0 1 1 0 1 0 0 0 1 1 0 0
0 0 1 0 1 1 0 1 1 0 1 0 0 0 1 1 0
0 0 0 1 0 1 1 0 1 1 0 1 0 0 0 1 1
1 0 0 0 1 0 1 1 0 1 1 0 1 0 0 0 1
1 1 0 0 0 1 0 1 1 0 1 1 0 1 0 0 0
0 1 1 0 0 0 1 0 1 1 0 1 1 0 1 0 0
0 0 1 1 0 0 0 1 0 1 1 0 1 1 0 1 0
0 0 0 1 1 0 0 0 1 0 1 1 0 1 1 0 1
1 0 0 0 1 1 0 0 0 1 0 1 1 0 1 1 0
0 1 0 0 0 1 1 0 0 0 1 0 1 1 0 1 1
1 0 1 0 0 0 1 1 0 0 0 1 0 1 1 0 1
1 1 0 1 0 0 0 1 1 0 0 0 1 0 1 1 0
```

```
Graph B

17
0 0 0 0 0 1 0 1 1 0 1 0 1 1 1 1 0
0 0 1 1 1 0 0 1 0 0 0 1 1 0 1 1 0
0 1 0 0 1 1 1 0 0 0 1 1 0 1 1 0 0
0 1 0 0 1 1 0 1 1 1 0 0 0 0 1 0 1
0 1 1 1 0 0 0 0 1 1 1 0 0 1 0 1 0
1 0 1 1 0 0 1 1 0 1 0 0 0 1 1 0 0
0 0 1 0 0 1 0 1 0 1 1 1 0 0 0 1 1
1 1 0 1 0 1 1 0 1 0 0 1 0 0 0 1 0
1 0 0 1 1 0 0 1 0 0 1 1 0 1 0 0 1
0 0 0 1 1 1 1 0 0 0 0 0 1 1 0 1 1
1 0 1 0 1 0 1 0 1 0 0 0 0 0 1 1 1
0 1 1 0 0 0 1 1 1 0 0 0 1 1 0 0 1
1 1 0 0 0 0 0 0 0 1 0 1 0 1 1 1 1
1 0 1 0 1 1 0 0 1 1 0 1 1 0 0 0 0
1 1 1 1 0 1 0 0 0 0 1 0 1 0 0 0 1
1 1 0 0 1 0 1 1 0 1 1 0 1 0 0 0 0
0 0 0 1 0 0 1 0 1 1 1 1 1 0 1 0 0
```

The algorithm finds an explicit isomorphism, shown below.

Figure 7.3. The Ramsey graphs are isomorphic

7.4. Example. We run the program on isomorphic Dodecahedron **[6]** graphs A and B as input:

```
Graph A

20
 0 1 0 0 1 0 0 0 0 0 0 0 0 1 0 0 0 0 0 0
 1 0 1 0 0 0 0 0 0 0 0 1 0 0 0 0 0 0 0 0
 0 1 0 1 0 0 0 0 0 1 0 0 0 0 0 0 0 0 0 0
 0 0 1 0 1 0 0 1 0 0 0 0 0 0 0 0 0 0 0 0
 1 0 0 1 0 1 0 0 0 0 0 0 0 0 0 0 0 0 0 0
 0 0 0 0 1 0 1 0 0 0 0 0 0 0 1 0 0 0 0 0
 0 0 0 0 0 1 0 1 0 0 0 0 0 0 0 1 0 0 0 0
 0 0 0 1 0 0 1 0 1 0 0 0 0 0 0 0 0 0 0 0
 0 0 0 0 0 0 0 1 0 1 0 0 0 0 0 0 1 0 0 0
 0 0 1 0 0 0 0 0 1 0 1 0 0 0 0 0 0 0 0 0
 0 0 0 0 0 0 0 0 1 0 1 0 0 0 0 0 0 1 0 0
 0 1 0 0 0 0 0 0 0 0 1 0 1 0 0 0 0 0 0 0
 0 0 0 0 0 0 0 0 0 0 0 1 0 1 0 0 0 0 0 1
 1 0 0 0 0 0 0 0 0 0 0 0 1 0 1 0 0 0 0 0
 0 0 0 0 0 1 0 0 0 0 0 0 0 1 0 1 0 0 0 0
 0 0 0 0 0 0 1 0 0 0 0 0 0 0 1 0 1 0 0 1
 0 0 0 0 0 0 0 0 1 0 0 0 0 0 0 1 0 1 0 0
 0 0 0 0 0 0 0 0 0 1 0 0 0 0 0 0 1 0 1 0
 0 0 0 0 0 0 0 0 0 0 1 0 0 0 0 0 0 1 0 1
 0 0 0 0 0 0 0 0 0 0 0 0 1 0 0 1 0 0 1 0
```

26

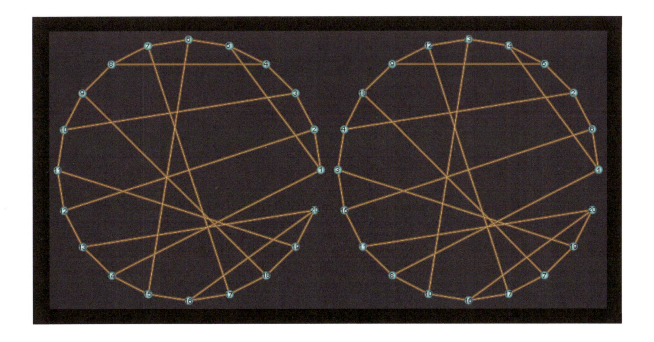

```
Graph B

20
 0 0 0 0 0 1 0 1 0 0 0 0 0 1 0 0 0 0 0 0
 0 0 0 1 1 1 0 0 0 0 0 0 0 0 0 0 0 0 0 0
 0 0 0 1 0 0 0 0 0 0 0 0 0 0 1 0 0 0 1 0
 0 1 1 0 0 0 0 0 0 0 0 0 0 0 0 0 0 1 0 0
 0 1 0 0 0 0 0 0 1 0 0 0 0 1 0 0 0 0 0 0
 1 1 0 0 0 0 0 0 0 0 0 0 0 0 1 0 0 0 0 0
 0 0 0 0 0 0 0 0 0 0 0 0 0 0 0 0 1 1 1 0
 1 0 0 0 0 0 0 0 0 1 1 0 0 0 0 0 0 0 0 0
 0 0 0 0 1 0 0 0 0 0 0 0 1 0 0 0 0 1 0 0
 0 0 0 0 0 0 1 0 0 0 0 1 0 0 1 0 0 0 0 0
 0 0 0 0 0 0 0 1 0 0 0 0 0 1 0 0 0 0 0 1
 0 0 0 0 0 0 0 0 1 0 0 0 1 0 0 0 1 0 0 0
 0 0 0 0 0 0 0 0 0 1 0 1 0 1 0 0 0 0 0 0
 1 0 0 0 1 0 0 0 0 0 0 0 0 0 0 1 0 0 0 0
 0 0 1 0 0 1 0 0 0 0 1 0 0 0 0 0 0 0 0 0
 0 0 0 0 0 0 0 0 1 0 0 0 0 0 0 0 0 1 0 1
 0 0 0 0 0 0 1 0 0 0 0 1 0 0 0 1 0 0 0 0
 0 0 0 1 0 0 1 0 1 0 0 0 0 0 0 0 0 0 0 0
 0 0 1 0 0 0 1 0 0 0 0 0 0 0 0 0 0 0 0 1
 0 0 0 0 0 0 0 0 0 0 1 0 0 0 0 1 0 0 1 0
```

The algorithm finds an explicit isomorphism, shown below.

Figure 7.4. *The Dodecahedron graphs are isomorphic*

27

7.5. Example. We run the program on isomorphic Coxeter [8] graphs A and B as input:

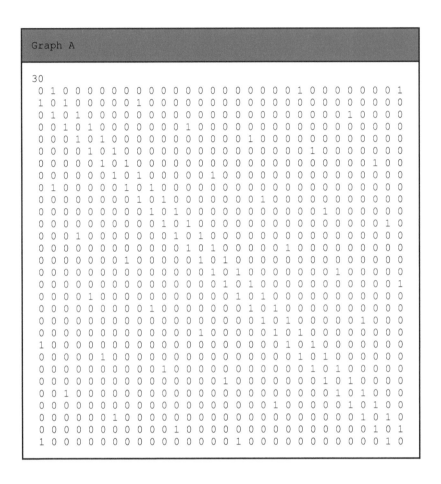

```
Graph A

30
 0 1 0 0 0 0 0 0 0 0 0 0 0 0 0 0 0 0 0 0 0 1 0 0 0 0 0 0 0 1
 1 0 1 0 0 0 0 1 0 0 0 0 0 0 0 0 0 0 0 0 0 0 0 0 0 0 0 0 0 0
 0 1 0 1 0 0 0 0 0 0 0 0 0 0 0 0 0 0 0 0 0 0 1 0 0 0 0 0 0 0
 0 0 1 0 1 0 0 0 0 0 0 1 0 0 0 0 0 0 0 0 0 0 0 0 0 0 0 0 0 0
 0 0 0 1 0 1 0 0 0 0 0 0 0 0 0 1 0 0 0 0 0 0 0 0 0 0 0 0 0 0
 0 0 0 0 1 0 1 0 0 0 0 0 0 0 0 0 0 0 1 0 0 0 0 0 0 0 0 0 0 0
 0 0 0 0 0 1 0 1 0 0 0 0 0 0 0 0 0 0 0 0 0 0 0 0 0 1 0 0 0 0
 0 0 0 0 0 0 1 0 1 0 0 0 0 1 0 0 0 0 0 0 0 0 0 0 0 0 0 0 0 0
 0 1 0 0 0 0 0 1 0 1 0 0 0 0 0 0 0 0 0 0 0 0 0 0 0 0 0 0 0 0
 0 0 0 0 0 0 0 0 1 0 1 0 0 0 0 0 1 0 0 0 0 0 0 0 0 0 0 0 0 0
 0 0 0 0 0 0 0 0 0 1 0 1 0 0 0 0 0 0 0 0 1 0 0 0 0 0 0 0 0 0
 0 0 0 0 0 0 0 0 0 0 1 0 1 0 0 0 0 0 0 0 0 0 0 0 0 0 0 1 0 0
 0 0 0 1 0 0 0 0 0 0 0 1 0 1 0 0 0 0 0 0 0 0 0 0 0 0 0 0 0 0
 0 0 0 0 0 0 0 0 0 0 0 0 1 0 1 0 0 0 0 0 1 0 0 0 0 0 0 0 0 0
 0 0 0 0 0 0 1 0 0 0 0 0 0 1 0 1 0 0 0 0 0 0 0 0 0 0 0 0 0 0
 0 0 0 0 0 0 0 0 0 0 0 0 0 0 1 0 1 0 0 0 0 0 0 1 0 0 0 0 0 0
 0 0 0 0 0 0 0 0 0 0 0 0 0 0 0 1 0 1 0 0 0 0 0 0 0 0 0 0 0 1
 0 0 0 0 1 0 0 0 0 0 0 0 0 0 0 0 1 0 1 0 0 0 0 0 0 0 0 0 0 0
 0 0 0 0 0 0 0 0 0 1 0 0 0 0 0 0 0 1 0 1 0 0 0 0 0 0 0 0 0 0
 0 0 0 0 0 0 0 0 0 0 0 0 0 0 0 0 0 0 1 0 1 0 0 0 0 0 1 0 0 0
 0 0 0 0 0 0 0 0 0 0 0 1 0 0 0 0 0 0 0 1 0 1 0 0 0 0 0 0 0 0
 1 0 0 0 0 0 0 0 0 0 0 0 0 0 0 0 0 0 0 0 1 0 1 0 0 0 0 0 0 0
 0 0 0 0 0 1 0 0 0 0 0 0 0 0 0 0 0 0 0 0 0 1 0 1 0 0 0 0 0 0
 0 0 0 0 0 0 0 0 0 1 0 0 0 0 0 0 0 0 0 0 0 0 1 0 1 0 0 0 0 0
 0 0 0 0 0 0 0 0 0 0 0 0 0 0 0 1 0 0 0 0 0 0 0 1 0 1 0 0 0 0
 0 0 1 0 0 0 0 0 0 0 0 0 0 0 0 0 0 0 0 0 0 0 0 0 1 0 1 0 0 0
 0 0 0 0 0 0 0 0 0 0 0 0 0 0 0 0 0 0 0 1 0 0 0 0 0 1 0 1 0 0
 0 0 0 0 0 0 1 0 0 0 0 0 0 0 0 0 0 0 0 0 0 0 0 0 0 0 1 0 1 0
 0 0 0 0 0 0 0 0 0 0 0 0 1 0 0 0 0 0 0 0 0 0 0 0 0 0 0 1 0 1
 1 0 0 0 0 0 0 0 0 0 0 0 0 0 0 0 1 0 0 0 0 0 0 0 0 0 0 0 1 0
```

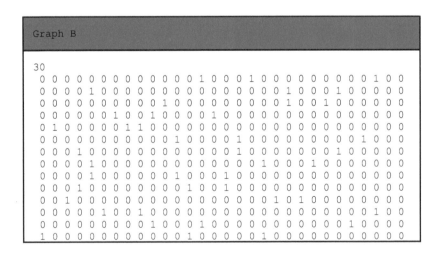

```
Graph B

30
 0 0 0 0 0 0 0 0 0 0 0 1 0 0 1 0 0 0 0 0 0 0 0 0 1 0 0
 0 0 0 0 1 0 0 0 0 0 0 0 0 0 0 0 0 1 0 0 1 0 0 0 0 0
 0 0 0 0 0 0 0 0 1 0 0 0 0 0 0 0 1 0 0 1 0 0 0 0 0 0
 0 0 0 0 0 1 0 0 1 0 0 0 1 0 0 0 0 0 0 0 0 0 0 0 0 0
 0 1 0 0 0 0 1 1 0 0 0 0 0 0 0 0 0 0 0 0 0 0 0 0 0 0
 0 0 0 0 0 0 0 0 0 0 1 0 0 0 1 0 0 0 0 0 0 0 1 0 0 0
 0 0 0 1 0 0 0 0 0 0 0 0 0 0 1 0 0 0 0 0 1 0 0 0 0 0
 0 0 0 0 1 0 0 0 0 0 0 0 0 0 1 0 0 1 0 0 0 0 0 0 0 0
 0 0 0 0 1 0 0 0 0 0 1 0 0 1 0 0 0 0 0 0 0 0 0 0 0 0
 0 0 0 1 0 0 0 0 0 0 0 1 0 0 1 0 0 0 0 0 0 0 0 0 0 0
 0 0 1 0 0 0 0 0 0 0 0 0 0 0 0 0 1 0 1 0 0 0 0 0 0 0
 0 0 0 0 0 1 0 0 1 0 0 0 0 0 0 0 0 0 0 0 0 0 1 0 0
 0 0 0 0 0 0 0 0 1 0 0 1 0 0 0 0 0 0 0 0 0 0 1 0 0 0
 1 0 0 0 0 0 0 0 0 0 0 1 0 0 0 0 0 1 0 0 0 0 0 0 0 0
```

28

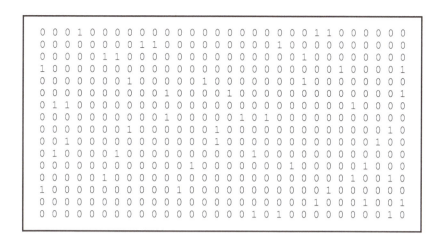

```
0 0 0 1 0 0 0 0 0 0 0 0 0 0 0 0 0 0 0 0 0 0 0 1 1 0 0 0 0 0
0 0 0 0 0 0 0 0 1 1 0 0 0 0 0 0 0 0 0 1 0 0 0 0 0 0 0 0 0 0
0 0 0 0 0 1 1 0 0 0 0 0 0 0 0 0 0 0 0 0 1 0 0 0 0 0 0 0 0 0
1 0 0 0 0 0 0 0 0 0 0 0 0 0 0 0 0 0 0 0 0 0 1 0 0 0 0 0 0 1
0 0 0 0 0 0 0 1 0 0 0 0 0 1 0 0 0 0 0 0 1 0 0 0 0 0 0 0 0 0
0 0 0 0 0 0 0 0 0 0 1 0 0 0 0 1 0 0 0 0 0 0 0 0 0 0 0 0 0 1
0 1 1 0 0 0 0 0 0 0 0 0 0 0 0 0 0 0 0 0 0 0 0 1 0 0 0 0
0 0 0 0 0 0 0 0 0 1 0 0 0 0 0 0 1 0 1 0 0 0 0 0 0 0 0 0 0 0
0 0 0 0 0 0 0 1 0 0 0 0 0 1 0 0 0 0 0 0 0 0 0 0 0 0 0 1 0
0 0 1 0 0 0 0 0 0 0 0 0 0 1 0 0 0 0 0 0 0 0 0 0 0 0 1 0 0
0 1 0 0 0 0 1 0 0 0 0 0 0 0 0 0 1 0 0 0 0 0 0 0 0 0 0 0 0
0 0 0 0 0 0 0 0 0 0 1 0 0 0 0 0 0 0 1 0 0 0 0 0 1 0 0 0
0 0 0 0 0 1 0 0 0 0 0 0 0 0 0 0 0 0 0 0 0 0 1 0 0 1 0
1 0 0 0 0 0 0 0 0 0 1 0 0 0 0 0 0 0 0 0 0 0 1 0 0 0 0 0
0 0 0 0 0 0 0 0 0 0 0 0 0 0 0 0 0 0 0 0 1 0 0 0 1 0 0 1
0 0 0 0 0 0 0 0 0 0 0 0 0 0 0 1 0 1 0 0 0 0 0 0 0 0 0 1 0
```

The algorithm finds an explicit isomorphism, shown below.

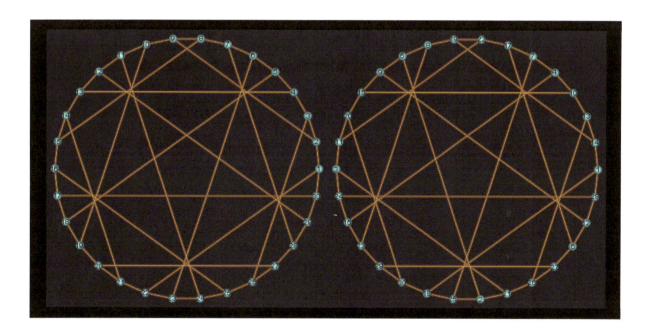

Figure 7.5. *The Coxeter graphs are isomorphic*

7.6. Example. We run the program on nonisomorphic Praust [9] graphs A and B as input:

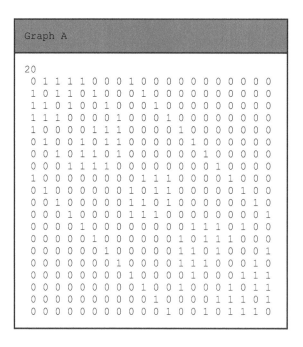

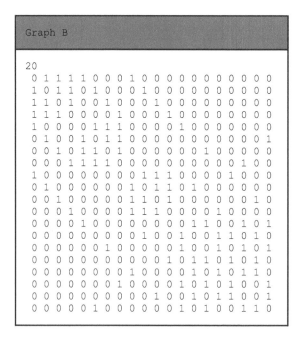

Graph A and Graph B have the same sign frequency vectors in lexicographic order, so their structure is very similar. The algorithm determines that the graphs are not isomorphic, shown below.

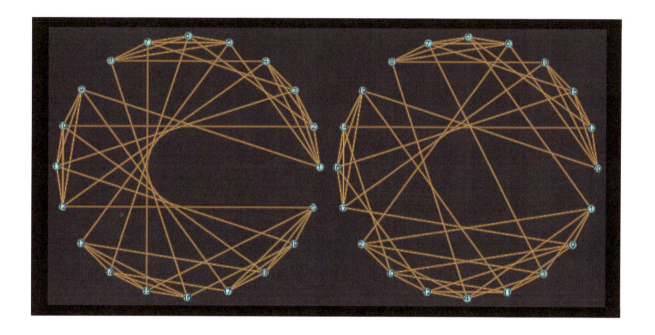

Figure 7.6. The Praust graphs are not isomorphic

7.7. Example. We run the program on nonisomorphic Mathon **[10]** graphs A and B as input:

Graph A

```
25
0 0 0 0 0 0 0 0 0 0 1 1 1 1 1 1 0 0 0 0 0 0 0 0 0
0 0 0 0 0 0 0 0 0 0 1 1 0 0 0 0 1 1 1 1 0 0 0 0 0
0 0 0 0 0 0 0 0 0 0 1 0 1 0 0 0 1 0 0 0 1 1 1 0 0
0 0 0 0 0 0 0 0 0 0 1 0 0 1 0 0 0 1 0 0 1 0 0 1 1
0 0 0 0 0 0 0 0 0 0 1 1 0 0 0 0 0 1 0 0 1 0 1 1 0
0 0 0 0 0 0 0 0 0 0 1 0 0 1 0 0 1 0 0 1 1 0 1 1 0
0 0 0 0 0 0 0 0 0 0 0 1 0 0 1 0 1 0 1 0 0 1 0 1 0
0 0 0 0 0 0 0 0 0 0 0 0 1 1 0 1 0 1 0 0 0 1 0 1 0
0 0 0 0 0 0 0 0 0 0 0 0 1 1 0 1 1 0 1 1 0 0 0 0 0
1 1 1 1 0 0 0 0 0 0 0 0 0 0 0 0 0 0 0 0 0 0 0 0 0
1 1 0 0 1 1 0 0 0 0 0 0 0 0 0 0 0 0 0 0 0 0 0 0 0
1 0 1 0 1 0 1 0 0 0 0 0 0 0 0 0 0 0 0 0 0 0 0 0 0
1 0 0 1 0 0 1 1 0 0 0 0 0 0 0 0 0 0 0 0 0 0 0 0 0
1 0 0 0 0 1 0 1 0 1 0 0 0 0 0 0 0 0 0 0 0 0 0 0 0
1 0 0 0 0 0 1 0 1 1 0 0 0 0 0 0 0 0 0 0 0 0 0 0 0
0 1 1 0 0 0 1 1 0 0 0 0 0 0 0 0 0 0 0 0 0 0 0 0 0
0 1 0 1 0 0 1 0 0 1 0 0 0 0 0 0 0 0 0 0 0 0 0 0 0
0 1 0 0 1 0 0 1 0 1 0 0 0 0 0 0 0 0 0 0 0 0 0 0 0
0 1 0 0 0 1 1 0 1 0 0 0 0 0 0 0 0 0 0 0 0 0 0 0 0
0 0 1 1 0 1 0 0 0 1 0 0 0 0 0 0 0 0 0 0 0 0 0 0 0
0 0 1 0 1 0 0 0 1 1 0 0 0 0 0 0 0 0 0 0 0 0 0 0 0
0 0 1 0 0 1 1 1 0 0 0 0 0 0 0 0 0 0 0 0 0 0 0 0 0
0 0 0 1 1 1 0 0 1 0 0 0 0 0 0 0 0 0 0 0 0 0 0 0 0
0 0 0 1 1 0 1 1 0 0 0 0 0 0 0 0 0 0 0 0 0 0 0 0 0
0 0 0 1 1 0 1 1 0 0 0 0 0 0 0 0 0 0 0 0 0 0 0 0 0
```

Graph B

```
25
0 0 0 0 0 0 0 0 0 0 1 1 1 1 1 1 0 0 0 0 0 0 0 0 0
0 0 0 0 0 0 0 0 0 0 1 1 0 0 0 0 1 1 1 1 0 0 0 0 0
0 0 0 0 0 0 0 0 0 0 1 0 1 0 0 0 1 0 0 0 1 1 1 0 0
0 0 0 0 0 0 0 0 0 0 1 0 0 1 0 0 0 1 0 0 1 0 0 1 1
0 0 0 0 0 0 0 0 0 0 1 1 0 0 0 0 0 1 0 0 1 0 1 1 0
0 0 0 0 0 0 0 0 0 0 1 0 0 1 0 0 1 0 0 1 1 0 1 1 0
0 0 0 0 0 0 0 0 0 0 0 1 0 0 1 0 1 0 1 0 0 1 0 1 0
0 0 0 0 0 0 0 0 0 0 0 0 1 0 1 0 0 1 1 1 1 0 0 0 0
0 0 0 0 0 0 0 0 0 0 0 0 1 1 1 1 0 0 0 1 0 1 0 0 0
1 1 1 1 0 0 0 0 0 0 0 0 0 0 0 0 0 0 0 0 0 0 0 0 0
1 1 0 0 1 1 0 0 0 0 0 0 0 0 0 0 0 0 0 0 0 0 0 0 0
1 0 1 0 1 0 1 0 0 0 0 0 0 0 0 0 0 0 0 0 0 0 0 0 0
1 0 0 1 0 0 1 1 0 0 0 0 0 0 0 0 0 0 0 0 0 0 0 0 0
1 0 0 0 0 1 0 1 0 1 0 0 0 0 0 0 0 0 0 0 0 0 0 0 0
1 0 0 0 0 1 0 1 1 0 0 0 0 0 0 0 0 0 0 0 0 0 0 0 0
0 1 1 0 0 0 1 0 1 0 0 0 0 0 0 0 0 0 0 0 0 0 0 0 0
0 1 0 1 0 0 1 0 0 1 0 0 0 0 0 0 0 0 0 0 0 0 0 0 0
0 1 0 0 1 0 0 1 1 0 0 0 0 0 0 0 0 0 0 0 0 0 0 0 0
0 1 0 0 0 1 1 0 1 0 0 0 0 0 0 0 0 0 0 0 0 0 0 0 0
0 0 1 1 0 1 0 0 0 1 0 0 0 0 0 0 0 0 0 0 0 0 0 0 0
0 0 1 0 1 0 0 0 1 1 0 0 0 0 0 0 0 0 0 0 0 0 0 0 0
0 0 1 0 0 1 1 1 0 0 0 0 0 0 0 0 0 0 0 0 0 0 0 0 0
0 0 0 1 1 1 0 0 1 0 0 0 0 0 0 0 0 0 0 0 0 0 0 0 0
0 0 0 1 1 0 1 1 0 0 0 0 0 0 0 0 0 0 0 0 0 0 0 0 0
0 0 0 1 1 0 1 1 0 0 0 0 0 0 0 0 0 0 0 0 0 0 0 0 0
```

Graph A and Graph B have the same sign frequency vectors in lexicographic order, so their structure is very similar. The algorithm determines that the graphs are not isomorphic, shown below.

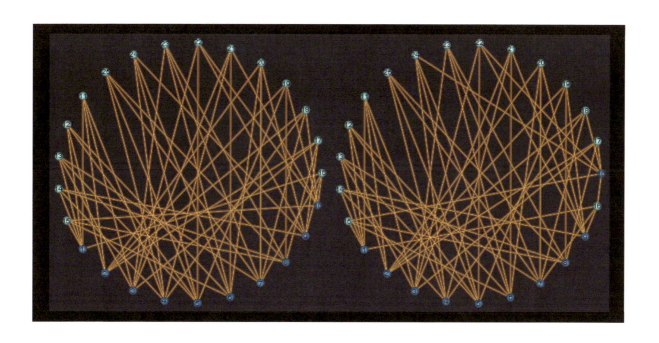

Figure 7.7. The Mathon graphs are not isomorphic

7.8. Example. We run the program on nonisomorphic Weisfeiler **[11]** graphs A and B as input:

```
Graph A

25
0 1 1 1 1 1 1 1 1 1 1 1 1 0 0 0 0 0 0 0 0 0 0 0 0
1 0 1 1 1 1 1 0 0 0 0 0 0 1 1 1 1 1 1 0 0 0 0 0 0
1 1 0 1 1 1 1 0 0 0 0 0 0 0 0 0 0 0 0 1 1 1 1 1 1
1 1 1 0 0 0 0 1 1 1 0 0 1 1 1 0 0 0 1 1 1 0 0 0
1 1 1 0 0 0 0 1 0 0 1 1 0 1 0 0 1 1 0 1 0 0 1 1 0
1 1 1 0 0 0 0 0 1 0 0 1 0 1 0 1 0 1 0 1 0 1 0 1 0 1
1 1 1 0 0 0 0 0 0 1 0 1 1 0 0 1 0 1 1 0 0 1 0 1 1 1
1 0 0 1 1 0 0 0 1 1 1 0 0 1 0 1 0 0 0 1 0 0 0 1 1 1
1 0 0 1 0 1 0 1 0 1 0 1 0 0 1 0 0 0 1 1 1 1 0 1 1 0 0
1 0 0 1 0 0 1 1 1 0 0 1 0 0 1 0 1 1 0 0 1 0 0 1 1
1 0 0 0 1 1 0 1 0 0 0 1 1 0 1 1 0 0 1 1 1 0 0 1 0
1 0 0 0 1 0 1 0 0 1 1 0 1 1 1 0 0 1 0 0 1 1 1 0 0
1 0 0 0 0 1 1 0 1 0 1 1 0 1 0 1 1 0 0 1 0 1 0 0 1
0 1 0 1 1 0 0 1 0 0 0 1 1 0 1 1 1 0 0 0 0 1 1 0 1
0 1 0 1 0 1 0 0 0 1 1 1 0 1 0 0 0 1 0 1 1 0 1 0
0 1 0 1 0 0 1 1 0 0 1 0 1 1 0 0 0 1 1 1 1 0 0 0 1
0 1 0 0 1 1 0 0 1 1 0 0 1 1 1 0 0 1 0 1 0 1 0 0 0 1 1
0 1 0 0 1 0 1 0 1 1 0 1 0 0 0 1 1 0 1 1 1 0 1 0 0
0 1 0 0 0 1 1 1 1 0 1 0 0 0 1 1 0 1 0 0 0 1 1 1 0
0 0 1 1 1 0 0 0 1 0 1 0 1 0 0 1 1 1 0 0 1 1 0 1 0
0 0 1 1 0 1 0 0 0 1 1 0 0 1 1 0 1 0 1 0 1 0 0 1 0 1
0 0 1 1 0 0 1 0 1 0 0 1 0 0 1 1 1 0 0 0 1 1 0 0 1 1 0
0 0 1 0 1 1 0 1 0 0 1 0 0 0 1 0 0 0 1 1 0 1 1 0 0 1
0 0 1 0 1 0 1 1 0 1 1 0 1 1 0 0 0 1 0 1 0 1 1 0 1 0 0 1
0 0 1 0 0 1 1 1 0 1 0 0 1 1 0 1 1 0 0 0 1 0 1 1 0
```

```
Graph B

25
0 1 1 1 1 1 1 1 1 1 1 1 1 0 0 0 0 0 0 0 0 0 0 0 0
1 0 1 1 1 1 1 0 0 0 0 0 0 1 1 1 1 1 1 0 0 0 0 0 0
1 1 0 1 1 1 1 0 0 0 0 0 0 0 0 0 0 0 0 1 1 1 1 1 1
1 1 1 0 0 0 0 1 1 1 0 0 0 1 1 1 0 0 0 1 1 1 0 0 0
1 1 1 0 0 0 0 1 0 0 1 1 0 1 0 0 1 1 0 1 0 0 1 1 0
1 1 1 0 0 0 0 0 1 0 1 0 1 0 1 0 1 0 1 0 1 0 1 0 1
1 1 1 0 0 0 0 0 0 1 0 1 1 0 0 1 0 1 1 0 0 1 0 1 1
1 0 0 1 1 0 0 0 1 1 1 0 0 1 0 1 0 0 1 0 0 0 1 1 1
1 0 0 1 0 1 0 1 0 1 0 1 0 1 0 0 1 0 1 1 0 0 0 1 1 0 1
1 0 0 1 0 0 1 1 1 0 0 0 1 0 0 0 1 1 1 1 0 0 1 0
1 0 0 0 1 1 0 1 0 0 0 1 1 1 1 0 0 0 1 0 1 1 0 1 0
1 0 0 0 1 0 1 0 1 0 1 0 1 0 1 0 1 1 0 1 0 1 0 1 1 0 0
1 0 0 0 0 1 1 0 0 1 1 1 0 1 1 0 1 1 0 0 1 1 0 0 0 1
0 1 0 1 1 0 0 1 0 1 0 1 0 0 1 1 1 0 0 1 1 0 0 1 1
0 1 0 1 0 1 0 0 1 1 0 0 1 1 0 0 1 1 0 1 1 0 1 0 1 0
0 1 0 1 0 0 1 1 0 0 0 1 1 1 1 0 0 0 1 1 0 0 1 0 1
0 1 0 0 1 1 0 0 1 1 0 0 1 1 1 0 0 1 0 1 0 0 0 1 1
0 1 0 0 1 0 1 0 1 1 0 1 0 1 0 1 0 0 1 0 1 0 1 1 1 0 0
0 1 0 0 0 1 1 1 0 1 1 1 0 0 0 1 1 0 1 0 0 1 0 1 1 0
0 0 1 1 1 0 0 0 0 1 0 1 1 0 1 1 1 0 0 0 1 0 1 1 0
0 0 1 1 0 1 0 0 0 1 1 0 1 1 0 0 0 1 1 1 0 0 1 1 1 0 0
0 0 1 1 0 0 1 0 1 0 1 1 0 1 1 0 1 1 0 0 1 0 0 1 0 0 1 1
0 0 1 0 1 1 0 1 1 0 1 1 0 0 1 0 0 0 1 0 1 1 1 1 0 0 0 1
0 0 1 0 1 0 1 1 0 1 1 0 1 1 0 0 0 1 0 1 0 1 1 0 1 0 0 1
0 0 1 0 0 1 1 1 1 1 0 0 0 1 1 0 1 1 0 0 0 0 1 1 1 0
```

Graph A and Graph B have different sign frequency vectors in lexicographic order. The algorithm determines that the graphs are not isomorphic, shown below.

Figure 7.8. The Weisfeiler graphs are not isomorphic

7.9. Example. We run the program on nonisomorphic Siberian [12] graphs A and B as input:

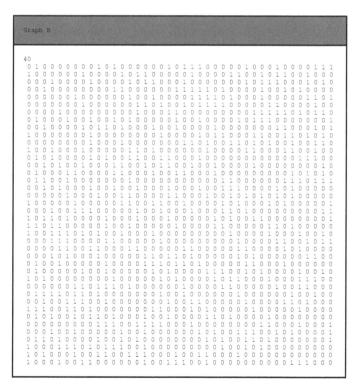

Graph A and Graph B have the same sign frequency vectors in lexicographic order, so their structure is very similar. The algorithm determines that the graphs are not isomorphic, shown below.

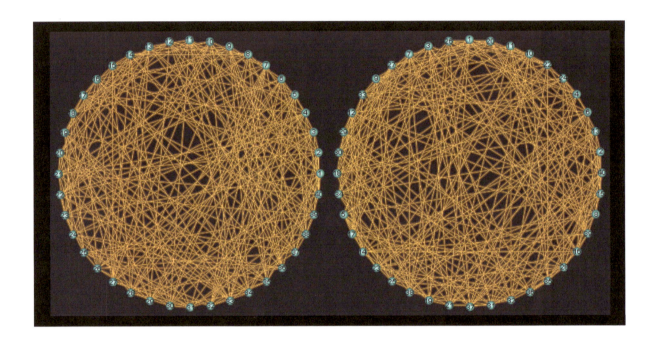

Figure 7.9. The Siberian graphs are not isomorphic

References

[1] Ashay Dharwadker and Shariefuddin Pirzada, *Graph Theory*, Orient Longman and Universities Press of India, 2008.

[2] John-Tagore Tevet, *Recognition of the Structure, Symmetry and Systems of Graphs*, Baltic Horizons, No. 8 (107), Special Issue Dedicated to 270 Years of Graph Theory, 2007.

[3] E. W. Dijkstra, *A note on two problems in connexion with graphs*, Numerische Mathematik, 1, 1959.

[4] P. Turán, *An extremal problem in graph theory*, Mat. Fiz. Lapok, 1941.

[5] J. Petersen, *Die Theorie der regulären Graphen*, Acta Math., 1891.

[6] Plato, *Timaeaus*, circa 350 B.C.

[7] F.P. Ramsey, *On a problem of formal logic*, Proc. London Math. Soc., 1930.

[8] H.S.M. Coxeter and W.T. Tutte, *The Chords of the Non-Ruled Quadratic in PG(3,3)*, Canad. J. Math., 1958.

[9] John-Tagore Tevet, *Constructive Representation of Graphs: A Selection of Examples*, S.E.R.R., Tallinn, 2008.

[10] R. Mathon, *Sample graphs for isomorphism testing*, Proc. 9th S-E. Conf. Combinatorics, Graph Theory and Computing, 1980.

[11] B. Weisfeiler, *On Construction and Identification of Graphs*, Springer Lecture Notes Math., 558, 1976.

[12] M. Netchepurenko et al., *Algorithms and programs for solution of problems in graphs and networks*, Novosibirsk, 1990.

www.ingramcontent.com/pod-product-compliance
Lightning Source LLC
Chambersburg PA
CBHW041425050326

40689CB00002B/654